THE BIBLE CURE®

FOR

HIGH BLOOD PRESSURE

DON COLBERT, M.D.

SILOAM PRESS

Living in Health—Body, Mind and Spirit

Library of Congress Catalog Card Number: 00-193613
International Standard Book Number: 0-88419-747-6

This book is not intended to provide medical advice or to take the place of medical advice and treatment from your personal physician. Readers are advised to consult their own doctors or other qualified health professionals regarding the treatment of their medical problems. Neither the publisher nor the author takes any responsibility for any possible consequences from any treatment, action or application of medicine, supplement, herb or preparation to any person reading or following the information in this book. If readers are taking prescription medications, they should consult with their physicians and not take themselves off of medicines to start supplementation without the proper supervision of a physician.

01 02 03 04 05 8 7 6 5 4 3 2
Printed in the United States of America

Discover Strength to Defeat High Blood Pressure

God intends to stop high blood pressure from weakening your body and robbing your health. He promises to greatly strengthen your life in every way. The Bible says, "God is awesome in his sanctuary. The God of Israel gives power and strength to his people. Praise be to God!" (Ps. 68:35).

Do you have high blood pressure? It can be a subtle and dangerous enemy. But God promises to strengthen your heart. His Word says, "My health may fail, and my spirit may grow weak, but God remains the strength of my heart; he is mine forever" (Ps. 73:26).

If you've been told that your blood pressure is too high, then I have good news for you. You don't have to face it alone. God promises to walk with you until you defeat it. He will get you through this, and with His powerful help you will overcome it!

A Dangerous
High Blood Pressure Epidemic

America is experiencing a high blood pressure epidemic. The statistics are alarming. High blood pressure—or hypertension—impacts the lives of about 50 million American adults. That means that approximately one out of four people, or one in every three adults, in this country have high blood pressure. The impact of all of this is alarming.

Cardiovascular disease is a killer that takes the lives of more than a million Americans every year. About half of all Americans will die of some form of cardiovascular disease. And high blood pressure is a primary reason for these deaths.

But this killer is extremely subtle. Most people never experience any symptoms from high blood pressure until it's advanced. So, about a third of the people who have high blood pressure don't even know it!

High blood pressure triples your risk of having a heart attack. It also increases your chances of having a stroke. About 70 percent of stroke victims have hypertension. Strokes are the third

leading killer of Americans, and they are the
number one cause of long-term disability.

Among other dangers, high blood pressure
can also lead to memory loss, dementia and even
Alzheimer's disease. Hypertension also damages
the kidneys, leading to kidney failure.

A Bold, New Approach

With the help of the practical and faith-inspiring
wisdom contained in this Bible Cure booklet,
you never have to experience high blood pressure. You can reverse high blood pressure
through the power of good nutrition, healthy
lifestyle choices, exercise, vitamins and supplements, and most importantly of all, through the
power of dynamic faith.

You don't have to suffer the debilitating consequences of high blood pressure. With God's
grace, health and joy await you at the end of
your days!

As you read this book, prepare to win the
battle against high blood pressure. This Bible
Cure booklet is filled with practical steps, hope,
encouragement and valuable information on how
to develop a healthy, empowered lifestyle. In this
book, you will

*uncover God's divine plan of health
for body, soul and spirit
through modern medicine, good nutrition
and the medicinal power
of Scripture and prayer.*

You will also discover life-changing scriptures throughout this booklet that will strengthen and encourage you.

As you read, apply and trust God's promises, you will also uncover powerful Bible Cure prayers to help you line up your thoughts and feelings with God's plan of divine health for you—a plan that includes living victoriously. In this Bible Cure booklet, you will find powerful insight in the following chapters:

1 Building Strength Through
   Understanding 1
2 Building Strength Through Nutrition . . . 14
3 Building Strength Through Exercise
   and Lifestyle Changes 31
4 Building Strength Through
   Supplements 39
5 Building Strength Through Dynamic
   Faith 57

You can confidently take the natural and spiritual steps outlined in this book to combat and defeat high blood pressure forever. It is my prayer that these practical suggestions for health, nutrition and fitness will bring wholeness to your life—body, soul and spirit. May they deepen your fellowship with God and strengthen your ability to worship and serve Him.

—DON COLBERT, M.D.

A BIBLE CURE PRAYER
FOR YOU

Dear God, thank You for the promise of Your strength. I ask You to make me able to receive all the wisdom, strength and power that You have for me. I acknowledge my need of You. You created my body and my mind, and without Your great power and wonderful wisdom, I'm helpless. But with Your help, I know that I will overcome. Amen.

Chapter 1

Building Strength
Through Understanding

Are you a wise and understanding person regarding high blood pressure? The Bible says, "Getting wisdom is the most important thing you can do! And whatever else you do, get good judgment" (Prov. 4:7).

According to God's Word, becoming a wise and understanding person is one of the most important things you can do. The benefits to your health and well-being cannot be measured.

Ignorance never protects you. The Bible says the opposite is actually true. "Understanding will keep you safe" (Prov. 2:11). The statistics about high blood pressure may seem absolutely astonishing to you. But with wisdom and understanding, you never have to be a statistic. So let's take a careful look at high blood pressure in an effort to gain greater understanding and wisdom about it.

How High Is Too High?

You may be wondering, *Just how high does my blood pressure need to be in order to be considered dangerous?*

If your blood pressure is greater than 140 over 90, it's too high. But be careful; you cannot determine that you have high blood pressure based upon one elevated reading. That's unless you have a reading that is off the charts, such as an extremely high systolic blood pressure reading of 210 and a diastolic reading of 120 or higher.

Otherwise, you must return to your physician's office for three different visits. At each visit, your blood pressure must be measured at least twice, one or more readings on each arm. Take a look at the

> *But those who wait on the LORD will find new strength. They will fly high on wings like eagles. They will run and not grow weary. They will walk and not faint.*
> —Isaiah 40:31

following chart to see how your own blood pressure ranks. These numbers are provided by the Joint National Committee on the Prevention, Detection, Evaluation and Treatment of High Blood Pressure.

How Do You Rank?

You have high blood pressure if your systolic measurement is greater than 140 and your diastolic measurement is greater than 90.

Stage One, or mild hypertension, reads:
- Systolic 140 to 159
- Diastolic 90 to 99

Stage Two, or moderate hypertension, reads:
- Systolic 160 to 179
- Diastolic 100 to 109

Stage Three, or severe hypertension, reads:
- Systolic greater than 180
- Diastolic greater than 110

A Few Tips

Your blood pressure rises and falls easily throughout the day. To be sure you get an accurate reading, here are a few tips to remember:

- Don't drink any coffee or caffeinated beverages for at least thirty minutes

3

before you get your blood pressure checked.

- Don't smoke or drink any alcohol for at least thirty minutes before having your blood pressure taken.

- Sit quietly for several minutes before having your blood pressure checked.

- Talking can make your blood pressure rise, so don't talk while you are getting checked.

Here are some other factors that can influence your blood pressure:

- Diet
- Environment
- Physical activity
- Medication
- Stress
- Emotional upset

Take your blood pressure at home and keep a log of the readings.

Your Incredible Cardiovascular System

Your body is an amazing creation, and your cardiovascular system is an incredible product of God's creative genius. The Bible says, "You made all the delicate, inner parts of my body and knit me together in my mother's womb. Thank you for making me so wonderfully complex! Your workmanship is marvelous—and how well I know it" (Ps. 139:13–14).

Only the genius of a wonderful, divine Creator could have made you. Let's take a closer look at the amazing system of blood vessels and cells

> *He gives power to those who are tired and worn out; he offers strength to the weak.*
> —Isaiah 40:29

that make up your cardiovascular system.

Your cardiovascular system is composed of the heart and blood vessels. With each heartbeat, blood is released from the left ventricle into the aorta, which is a very large blood vessel that then transports the blood throughout the body. The heart is the pump, and the blood vessels are like pipes that circulate the blood.

In Deuteronomy 12:23, the Bible says that our life is in our blood, and it's really true. Your blood delivers oxygen and essential nutrients, which include vitamins, minerals, proteins, essential fats, sugars and hormones, to all the cells in your body. The blood also removes waste products. The blood is then returned to the heart through the veins. After that it is sent to the lungs to receive a fresh supply of oxygen. And the process starts all over again.

The average pulse, which is the average heart rate, is approximately seventy beats a minute. The human heart never gets a break. It has to work continually day and night. It beats about forty-two hundred times an hour and over a hundred thousand times a day, which is over thirty-seven million times a year. When your blood pressure is normal, this presents no stress to the heart. But if your blood pressure is elevated, your heart must begin to work harder to pump the blood.

With Every Beat of My Heart

If your heart has to work harder with every beat, over time it will actually become larger and larger. It's just like working out at a gym. When you lift weights and do curls, your muscles bulk up, becoming larger and larger. When the heart has to work harder, it actually grows larger, too.

That may be great for your biceps, but it's really bad for your heart. When the size of your heart increases, it leads to left ventricular hypertrophy. Let me explain what this is. As your heart gets larger, it requires more blood to nourish it. But when you have high blood pressure, your heart doesn't get the increased supply of blood it needs because high blood pressure also causes the blood vessels to become narrowed. This reduces the supply of blood to the heart.

This is why high blood pressure places you at greater risk of experiencing a heart attack and sudden death. Also, as the heart enlarges, it can become weaker since it doesn't have the strength to pump effectively against the elevated blood pressure. You may eventually develop congestive heart failure, in which the heart becomes so weak that fluid begins to accumulate in the legs and in the lungs.

Wreaking Havoc on Your Arteries

High blood pressure also damages the arteries. Healthy arteries are very flexible and elastic, but high blood pressure can lead to arteriosclerosis, which is hardening of the arteries.

Here's how it works. With high blood pressure, the walls of the arteries become thick and stiff.

High blood pressure or hypertension also causes atherosclerosis. In atherosclerosis the inner wall of the artery is actually damaged, usually by high blood pressure. Platelets adhere to the site of injury, and fatty deposits begin to collect there. As fatty deposits begin to accumulate, they form plaque, which eventually hardens.

The buildup of plaque can decrease blood flow even more. If the affected blood vessel is in the heart, it can lead to a heart attack. If it is in the brain, it can lead to a stroke.

Continued high blood pressure can also weaken blood vessels, leading to aneurysms. An aneurysm is a weakening or bulging in the wall of

> *God is awesome in his sanctuary. The God of Israel gives power and strength to his people.*
> —PSALM 68:35

an artery. An aneurysm may rupture, causing a person to bleed to death. The most common areas where aneurysms occur are in an artery in the brain and in the abdominal aorta.

Causes of Hypertension

There are two main types of high blood pressure: essential and secondary hypertension. About 95 percent of patients with hypertension have essential hypertension. I believe that most cases of essential hypertension are caused by lifestyle, obesity, excessive stress and nutritional deficiencies. Secondary hypertension, on the other hand, is usually caused by kidney disease, medications and drugs (such as birth control pills and cocaine) and adrenal disorders. That, however, is rare, only affecting about 5 percent of people with hypertension.

Are You at Risk?

Even though the actual cause of high blood pressure is unknown, risk factors can dramatically increase your chances of developing it. You have a great deal of control over some of these risk factors, but not all. It's impossible to have control over some risk factors. Listed below are some of them.

Risk Factors You Cannot Control

Your family history

If both of your parents had hypertension, there is a 60 percent chance that you will develop it. If only one parent had hypertension, you still have a 25 percent chance of developing it yourself.

Your sex

Before age fifty, men are more likely to develop hypertension. However, after age fifty, hypertension is more common in women than in men.

Your age

As you get older, your risk of developing hypertension increases.

Your race

African Americans develop hypertension twice as often as whites. Mexicans, Cubans and Puerto Ricans are also more prone to develop hypertension.

Secondary Causes of High Blood Pressure

Secondary hypertension can be cured most of the time. Causes of secondary hypertension include kidney diseases such as polycystic kidney disease and renal artery stenosis, which is a narrowing of the arteries that supply blood to the kidneys.

Since most high blood pressure falls under the category of essential hypertension, we will focus on modifying the risk factors that we can control.

Here's a list of main risk factors:

- Obesity
- Inactivity
- Stress
- Lifestyle factors
- Alcohol

- Smoking
- Nutritional factors

By modifying these risk factors, you should be able to control the majority of cases of mild and moderate hypertension.

Before you begin to make changes, it's very important to have a comprehensive physical exam that includes blood work, urinalysis and an EKG. Make sure that your doctor rules out any secondary causes of hypertension.

Conclusion

I trust that you've gained a little wisdom and insight into what high blood pressure is and why you or your loved one has it. In the face of these medical facts, your goal is to take advantage of the wealth of wisdom in God's Word and in the medical understanding with which God has blessed us. Most importantly, I encourage you to take hold of the healing power of Jesus Christ that He bought for you by His own sufferings.

A BIBLE CURE PRAYER
FOR YOU

Dear Lord, thank You that You are sup-
plying wisdom and understanding to my
life. With You on my side, I know I'm not
a statistic. I thank You for Your love and
favor in my life. I ask You for Your help to
develop a new lifestyle that will free my
destiny from the negative consequences
of high blood pressure. Most importantly,
Lord, help me to understand and to lay
hold of the healing power of Jesus Christ
in my life. Amen.

Faith Builder

> He was pierced through for our transgres-
> sions, He was crushed for our iniquities; the
> chastening of our well-being fell upon Him,
> and by His scourging we are healed.
>
> —Isaiah 53:5, NAS

Write out this verse and insert your own name into it: "He was pierced through for _____'s transgressions, He was crushed for _____'s iniquities; the chastening of _____'s well-being fell upon Him, and by His scourging _____ is healed!"

Write out a personal prayer to Jesus Christ, thanking Him for exchanging His health for your pain. Thank Him for taking the power of sickness onto His own body so that He could purchase your healing from high blood pressure.

_____

_____

_____

_____

Chapter 2

Building Strength Through Nutrition

You are God's precious possession; His great favor is upon you. You are the apple of His eye. The Bible says, "For the Lord's portion is his people, Jacob his allotted inheritance . . . He shielded him and cared for him; he guarded him as the apple of his eye" (Deut. 32:9–10, NIV).

What a privilege it is to be chosen by God, selected by Him as the object of His love, His special care, His protection and His guidance! You are not a statistic, destined to suffer the debilitating effects of high blood pressure. God's special love and care for you include imparting wisdom to you and healing power to help you overcome hypertension.

That wisdom includes natural nutritional solutions that can turn high blood pressure around. Let's take a look.

What Is Your Bathroom Scale Trying to Tell You?

How long has it been since you have weighed yourself and felt good about it? Being overweight can double your risk of developing high blood pressure. In fact, obese individuals have a two to six times greater rate of hypertension than those with normal weight. You can see why obesity is also the most important risk factor related to hypertension.

Every pound of fat in your body needs miles of blood vessels to supply the fat with oxygen and nutrients. Too much blood and too many blood vessels lead to increased resist-

> *For troubles surround me— too many to count! They pile up so high I can't see my way out.*
> —PSALM 40:12

ance within the vessels. This adds more pressure on the arterial walls, driving up blood pressure. There is usually a direct relationship between weight and high blood pressure. As your weight increases, usually your blood pressure will increase also.

How Fat Is Obese?

Obesity is defined as being 20 percent above your ideal body weight or a body mass index (BMI) of 30 or more. Body mass index is a formula that uses your weight and height to determine if your weight is normal, overweight or obese. A BMI of 19–24 is healthy. A BMI of 25–29 is overweight, and a BMI of 30 or more is obese.

According to federal guidelines, a third of adults are overweight, and nearly 25 percent are obese. Not only does obesity increase your risk of having high blood pressure, but it also increases your risk of diabetes, stroke, heart disease and even cancer.

> *They will continue to grow stronger and each of them will appear before God in Jerusalem.*
> —PSALM 84:7

Hypertension is three times more common among obese patients (with BMI greater than 30) than in patients of normal weight. In over 70 percent of patients with hypertension, the high blood pressure is directly related to obesity.

Take a look at the body mass index chart in the following Bible Cure HealthFact to determine which category—normal, overweight or obese—you are in.

Body Mass Index

Too much body fat is an obvious warning sign. You can measure your body fat. Draw a line from your weight (left column) to your height (right column). Is your BMI (middle column) in the "healthy" range?

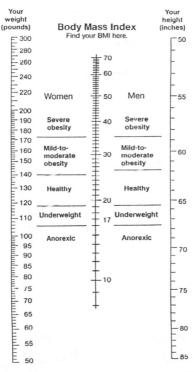

Your weight (pounds) — **Body Mass Index** Find your BMI here. — **Your height (inches)**

Women — Men

Severe obesity

Mild-to-moderate obesity

Healthy

Underweight

Anorexic

Losing weight and achieving a healthy BMI could save your life. In addition to helping you to beat high blood pressure, it will make you feel great about yourself again. Think of how wonderful it would feel to get into some of those slacks that have been pushed to the back of your closet for so long.

For natural and spiritual power to defeat obesity, read my booklet *The Bible Cure for Weight Loss and Muscle Gain*.

What Fruit Are You?

When it comes to high blood pressure, it's not only important to understand if you're overweight, but you should also be aware of *how* you're overweight. Let me explain.

Apple-shaped

Where is your body's excess fat located? This is critically important when it comes to high blood pressure. Do you have a few love handles on your tummy, abdomen and back? If you are a person with abdominal obesity, or central obesity, you are considered "apple-shaped."

If you are apple-shaped, you are much more likely to develop high blood pressure, diabetes, strokes and coronary artery disease. The reason is this: When your fat is mainly in your abdomen, it tends to accumulate in your arteries, leading to vascular disease.

Here's how you can determine if you have an apple shape. Simply measure the narrowest area around your waist and the widest area around your hips. Divide the measurement of your waist by the measurement of your hips. If this number is greater that 0.95 in men or greater than 0.8 in women, then you have an apple shape.

Pear-shaped

If your extra fat is stored in your thighs, hips and buttocks, you are "pear-shaped." This body shape is not nearly as dangerous as apple-shaped obesity.

Apple-Shaped Obesity

Many patients with apple-shaped obesity also tend to be insulin resistant. Insulin resistance is present in about half of those who have high blood pressure.

When you are insulin resistant, your cells do not properly respond to insulin. As you eat a meal with a lot of sugars or processed, refined starches, these sugars and starches break down into glucose, which is then absorbed into the bloodstream.

Glucose triggers the pancreas to secrete insulin. Insulin then causes glucose and other nutrients to be delivered into the cells. As glucose enters the cells, the glucose levels in the blood fall, which then signals the pancreas to stop producing insulin.

But in many obese patients these insulin receptors in the cells do not work properly. Therefore sufficient

> *Bless the LORD, who is my rock. He gives me strength for war and skill for battle.*
> —PSALM 144:1

amounts of glucose and nutrients do not reach the cells, which causes the glucose to remain in the blood. The high levels of blood glucose trigger the pancreas to continue secreting insulin. Now you have high levels of both glucose and insulin. Over time, this situation leads to Type 2 diabetes.

As insulin levels and blood sugars rise, deposits of fat in the abdomen are also more likely to break down and accumulate in the arteries. This usually leads to elevated cholesterol and triglyceride levels.

"X" Marks the Spot

The very worst scenario for high blood pressure is marked with an "X." When you have apple-shaped obesity, high blood pressure and abnormal glucose tolerance with elevated blood sugar, cholesterol and triglyceride levels, it's called "Syndrome X."

Individuals with these symptoms usually have low HDL cholesterol and elevated uric acid levels as well. Syndrome Xers are at high risk of developing both heart disease and Type 2 diabetes.

Half of those with hypertension also have insulin resistance, and many individuals with high blood pressure also have Syndrome X. Approximately 25 percent of Americans have some degree of Syndrome X. So you can see that it's vitally important to modify your diet, begin an exercise program and lose weight before you develop diabetes or cardiovascular disease.

Preventing Insulin Resistance

To prevent insulin resistance and Syndrome X, choose a diet of low-glycemic foods. These are foods that release glucose slowly into your bloodstream. This in turn lowers your insulin levels.

The glycemic index of a food simply refers to the rate at which blood glucose rises after a specific food is eaten.

High-glycemic foods cause a sudden rise in

both blood sugar and insulin, which can lead to insulin resistance, high blood pressure, obesity and diabetes.

A BIBLE CURE HEALTHFACT

Glycemic Index of Foods

EXTREMELY HIGH (GREATER THAN 100)

Corn flakes
Millet
Potato, baked, instant
Honey
Rice, instant, puffed
Bread, French
Carrots, cooked

GLYCEMIC STANDARD = 100 PERCENT

Bread, white

HIGH (80–100)

Bread, rye, wheat,
  whole meal
Grape Nuts
Muesli
Crispbread
Corn, sweet
Potato, broiled, mashed
Apricots
Banana
Mango
Pastry
Crackers
Shredded wheat
Tortilla, corn
Rice, brown, white
Raisins
Papaya
Candy bars
Cookies
Ice cream, low fat
Corn chips

MODERATELY HIGH (60–80)

Buckwheat
All Bran

Bread, rye, pumpernickel   Bulgur
Macaroni, white   Spaghetti, white, brown
Yams   Sweet potatoes
Green peas   Green peas (frozen)
Baked beans (canned)   Kidney beans (canned)
Fruit cocktail   Grapefruit juice
Orange juice   Pineapple juice
Pears (canned)   Grapes
Oatmeal cookies   Potato chips
Sponge cake

Moderate (40–60)

White beans   Tomato soup
Green peas, dried   Lima beans
Butter beans   Chickpeas (garbanzo)
Kidney beans   Black-eyed peas
Black beans   Apple juice
Orange   Apple
Pears   Milk
Yogurt

Low (less than 40)

Barley   Soybeans
Red lentils   Plums
Peaches   Peanuts
Fructose

Complex carbohydrates found in vegetables, whole grains and legumes do not have a high

23

glycemic index, and they also contain fiber. Fiber slows down the release of insulin in your bloodstream. So, avoid eating white bread, white rice, bagels, crackers, cookies and a lot of pasta.

Choose sprouted wheat bread such as Ezekiel bread and whole-grain bread. Slow-cooked oatmeal has a low glycemic index. Choosing lower glycemic foods will help you to lose weight, which in turn will help lower your blood pressure.

Freedom From Harmful Fats

If your diet is high in fats, it is probably contributing to high blood pressure. But not all fats are bad. In fact, some fats are very good for you. Bad fats that contribute to high blood pressure are saturated fats. These are found primarily in the following foods:

- Fatty cuts of meat such as beef, pork, ham, veal and lamb
- Eggs
- Whole-milk dairy products such as butter, cheese, whole milk and cream
- Oils such as coconut oil, vegetable shortening and palm kernel oil

Tips for Selecting Healthier Foods

When you select meats, choose the leanest cuts of meat such as fillet or tenderloin. Make sure that they are free-range meats. Also, peel the skin off chicken or turkey. Bake or broil your meat, and avoid all fried foods.

Choose low-fat dairy products such as skim milk, skim milk cheeses and low-fat yogurt. Eat an egg only a few times a week.

The Dangers of Hydrogenated Fats

Probably the most dangerous fats are hydrogenated fats. Hydrogenated fats like margarine and shortening contribute greatly to heart disease.

These dangerous fats raise cholesterol levels, and they are high in trans fatty acids. Most polyunsaturated vegetable oils such as corn oil, soybean oil, sunflower oil and safflower oil are partially hydrogenated to increase shelf life. Vegetable shortening and margarines are the most hydrogenated fats. Foods that are partially hydrogenated include potato chips, corn chips, crackers, cookies, cakes, pies, pastries, salad dressings and most frozen dinners.

Finding Good Fats

Good fats can actually help protect you from heart disease and hypertension. These good fats are essential fatty acids called Omega-3 and Omega-6 fatty acids.

Omega-6 fatty acids are found in grains, vegetable oils and nuts. Most Americans get plenty of these. Choose the cold-pressed vegetable oils in the health food store rather than the processed oils in the grocery store.

Nevertheless, many Americans are lacking in Omega-3 fatty acids, which can be found in flaxseed oil and cold-water fish such as salmon, herring, halibut, mackerel, tuna and sardines.

The Miracle of Omega-3 Fats

Omega-3 fatty acids work in your body to help to regulate blood pressure. They also help prevent blood platelets from sticking together, thus preventing blood clots. Omega-3 fatty acids also help to decrease both triglycerides and cholesterol levels.

Your Rx

Eat at least 4 ounces of cold-water fish such as

salmon or mackerel three times a week. Or take a 1000-milligram fish oil capsule twice a day, or 1 tablespoon flaxseed oil once a day or two capsules with each meal.

Monounsaturated fats are also very healthy, and include extra-virgin olive oil, almonds, canola oil and avocados.

A Hypertension-Busting Diet

Choose a diet with the following characteristics:

- Plenty of fruits and vegetables
- Low in the bad fats (saturated and hydro-genated fat)
- High in protective fat (fish oil and flaxseed oil)
- Foods with a lower glycemic index

This diet can help to reduce your blood pressure and even help you to lose weight.

Conclusion

Changing the way you eat can be the most difficult thing you ever do. But you're not alone. Never forget that you

> *The LORD is my strength and my song; he has become my victory.*
> —PSALM 118:14

may have an apple-shaped body, but you are still the apple of God's eye. He is ready and eager to give you the help you need to live a healthier, more joyful life. Choose to take Him at His Word. You won't be sorry!

A Bible Cure Prayer
FOR YOU

Dear Jesus, I make up my mind right now to choose to believe Your Word. I may not understand why, but Your Word says that You love me deeply, and despite my weaknesses and imperfections, I'm still the apple of Your eye. With Your help day in and day out, I will change my eating habits to ones that honor You and protect my health. In Jesus' name, amen.

Keep a Daily Food Diary

Date/ Weight	Breakfast	Snack	Lunch
/			
/			
/			
/			
/			
/			
/			
/			
/			

Make copies as needed

A BIBLE CURE PRESCRIPTION

Keep a Daily Food Diary

Snack	Dinner	Evening Snack

Make copies as needed

Chapter 3

Building Strength Through Exercise and Lifestyle Changes

Whether you realize it or not, you are a very privileged character. God not only sees you as an object of His love, but He also created you as the object of His special care. Here is another Bible verse that speaks of you as especially chosen by God: "Whoever touches you touches the apple of his eye" (Zech. 2:8, NIV).

What a wonderful privilege it is to know and recognize His amazing love and incredible care! He created you to be truly unique—one of a kind. And not only did He grace you with your life, but He also blessed your life with purpose. He will help you to understand and obtain the destiny He has for you.

Although diseases such as high blood pressure might try to get in the way of your destiny, it's also God's will to help you to overcome.

Developing a healthier lifestyle will help, and regular exercise, a natural remedy for high blood pressure, is an important part of that lifestyle. Let's examine the role of exercise and lifestyle changes in helping you to live in the destiny of favor that God has for you.

Changing the Way
You Think About Exercise

The American College of Sports Medicine reports that less than 10 percent of Americans exercise at the recommended level, and as many as 30 percent don't exercise at all.[1]

Regular aerobic exercise can lower your blood pressure as much as taking medications. It's a powerful, healthy alternative choice. Why risk the side effects of antihypertensive medications? Why not start an exercise program and watch your blood pressure decrease?

Perhaps you haven't been active in a long time, and you just dread the thought of joining an aerobics class or jogging. Don't try to change your lifestyle and your thinking all at once. Instead of planning to become a marathon runner overnight, why not just decide to take one small step at a time? It took a long time to develop your sedentary habits, and it may take a little time to retrain yourself.

Decide to start today by parking your car at the back of the parking lot and walking farther.

> *The joy of the* Lord *is your strength.*
> —Nehemiah 8:10

That's easy. In a couple of days, start taking the steps in the morning. Before the week is out, start taking the steps at lunch, too. By making little choices and taking small steps that lead to larger ones, you will become an active person before you know it.

The Benefits of Exercise

Moderate physical activity such as brisk walking can lower blood pressure in a number of different ways. First of all, regular physical activity makes the heart stronger so that the heart is able to pump more blood with less effort. Since the heart doesn't have to work as hard to pump blood, less force is thus exerted on the arteries, resulting in the lowering of blood pressure.

Regular exercise also stabilizes the blood sugar levels, which improves insulin sensitivity. Insulin resistance is an underlying factor for about half of those with hypertension.

You increase muscle and lose fat when you exercise regularly. Regular exercise also decreases stress and anxiety and promotes better sleep. Exercise causes your

> *For wisdom will enter your heart, and knowledge will fill you with joy.*
> —Proverbs 2:10

levels of good cholesterol, which is HDL, to increase. Therefore, it can significantly decrease the risk of atherosclerosis and hypertension.

The Surgeon General's Report on Physical Activity and Health stated, "Regular physical activity prevents or delays the development of high blood pressure, and exercise reduces blood pressure in people with hypertension."[2]

It's important to continue exercising on a regular basis to maintain these benefits. Soon after you stop exercising regularly, your blood pressure will return to its former level.

Working Out

To be really effective against high blood pressure, work up to a regular program of moderately intensive aerobic exercise three to five times a week for twenty to sixty minutes per workout.

I want to emphasize the importance of starting out slowly—only five or ten minutes at a time at low intensity. Gradually increase the time and intensity as your fitness improves.

In 1995, the American Heart Association and the American College of Sports Medicine issued new guidelines for physical activity. The new guidelines place more emphasis on the activity instead of the intensity, since studies have found that less-vigorous exercise was also effective.[3]

See Your Doctor

If you have multiple cardiovascular risk factors such as hypertension, a smoking history, high cholesterol or a strong family history of heart disease, I strongly recommend that you get a physical examination and undergo an exercise stress test before beginning an exercise program.

Every year in the U.S. about 75,000 Americans have a heart attack during or after vigorous exercise. These are generally people with a sedentary lifestyle or who have risk factors for heart attack. Even after your physician has medically cleared you for exercise, avoid intense exercise until your cardiovascular risk factors have been modified and your cardiovascular fitness has improved.

Individuals living in northern states generally

experience more incidents of heart attack while shoveling snow after heavy snow falls. But if you are young with mild hypertension and exercise moderately, your risk for heart attack is extremely low. In fact, researchers have found that fewer than ten individuals out of 100,000 will have a heart attack during exercise. Those who do suffer heart attacks are usually sedentary with other risk factors for heart disease, and they exercise too hard for their level of fitness.

If you experience tightness in the chest while exercising, chest pain or pain down the left arm or up into the jaw, rapid heartbeats, lightheadedness or severe shortness of breath, seek medical attention immediately. In addition, I strongly advise against exercising near heavy traffic since the carbon monoxide and air pollution can damage the heart and blood vessels.

Conclusion

Becoming a more active person will not only lower your blood pressure and protect your heart, but as you develop a healthier and more active lifestyle, you will discover many other powerful benefits. You will begin to feel better physically, mentally and emotionally. You will also begin to look better as you begin to lose weight and tone your muscles.

As you get started, remember that God is with you to help you. Whisper a prayer to Him for help whenever you need it. He will help you to stay motivated and keep at it. You will begin to experience the joy and excitement of your destiny as one who is highly favored by God as the apple of His eye!

A BIBLE CURE PRAYER
FOR YOU

Dear Lord, thank You for Your wonderful favor upon my life. Thank You that my life is more valuable to You than it is to me, and that You have made me the apple of Your eye. Thank You for planning a destiny for me that includes good health and a long, productive and blessed life. Help me to begin a new lifestyle of regular exercise and activity. Help me to be faithful and disciplined. In Jesus' name, amen.

A BIBLE CURE PRESCRIPTION

Check the lifestyle changes you plan to make:

❑ Exercise regularly.

I plan to begin a program of _____.

❑ Begin an aerobic program.

❑ Purchase fitness equipment for my home.

❑ Begin ballroom dancing or _____.

❑ Begin parking my car at the back of the lot

or _____.

Write your own prayer asking God for help in making these lifestyle changes.

_____

_____

Write a prayer of commitment asking God for His help in staying faithful to an exercise program.

_____

_____

Chapter 4

Building Strength Through Supplements

As part of God's great love and favor in your life, He has graced the world with everything you need to be healthy. The Bible says, "He causeth the grass to grow for the cattle, and herb for the service of man: that he may bring forth food out of the earth" (Ps. 104:14, KJV).

God has provided what your body needs to be healthy and fit. But too often our hectic eating habits, poor food choices and nutrient-depleted foods rob our bodies of the benefits God intended. Even so, God has still made provision for us, for He has promised to supply all of our needs. The Bible says, "You can be sure that God will take care of everything you need" (Phil. 4:19, THE MESSAGE). God is well aware of the time and circumstances in which we live, and in His great love for us He has provided for our care.

You may be thinking, *But how does this relate to supplements? Aren't these made by man?* They are, but the knowledge and understanding, as well as the materials, are all given by God. The Word of God says, "The earth is the LORD's, and everything in it. The world and all its people belong to him" (Ps. 24:1).

Even though much of the food we eat doesn't totally supply the vitamin and mineral requirements of our bodies, God has graced our world with the know-how to make up the lack. And when it comes to high blood pressure, supplements can make all the difference in the world.

Let's take a look at some supplements that are an essential part of your Bible cure for high blood pressure.

Battling Molecular Warfare

Taking supplements can greatly strengthen your body's ability to battle the devastating effects of free radicals. You probably don't realize it, but right now your cells are fighting a molecular atomic war. At this very moment, free radicals are bombarding your body, creating molecular havoc. Let me explain.

Free radicals are unstable molecules that

damage healthy cells like a kind of molecular shrapnel, creating chain reactions of cellular destruction. Free-radical damage also contributes to hypertension and atherosclerosis.

When high blood pressure goes untreated for too long, your arteries lose their elasticity and actually begin to harden. The hypertension causes shearing forces that injure the lining of the arterial walls, causing the buildup of even more plaque. More and more plaque builds up until arteries become blocked or you experience a heart attack.

That's why antioxidants are critically important. Like Patriot missiles, they stop these free-radical reactions and protect the lining of the blood vessels from further plaque buildup. Let's look at some of these powerful defenders.

Vitamin C

One of the most important antioxidants for the heart and blood vessels is vitamin C. Vitamin C helps to repair the damage done to the arteries from hypertension. It also prevents free-radical damage to the arteries. Vitamin C strengthens and restores elasticity to the blood vessels.

I recommend 500 to 1000 milligrams of vitamin C, preferably in buffered form, three times a day.

Vitamin E

This power-packed antioxidant can really decrease your risk of heart disease and hypertension. An eight-year study of nurses from Harvard University found that 41 percent of the 87,245 nurses who took 100 units of vitamin E daily for more than two years had fewer heart attacks. An impressive 41 percent registered a lower risk of heart disease than those who did not take the vitamin E supplement.[1]

Avoid synthetic vitamin E (which is DL-alpha-tocopherol). Instead, look for D-alpha-tocopherol. I recommend 400–800 IUs of vitamin E daily.

Coenzyme Q_{10}

Coenzyme Q_{10} is an incredible high-blood-pressure-busting antioxidant. In higher doses it is also very helpful for those with congestive heart failure and cardiomyopathy.

I normally place my hypertensive patients on 100 milligrams of coenzyme Q_{10} two times a day.

Lipoic acid

This unique substance is the only antioxidant with the unusual power to regenerate itself. Not only can it recycle itself, but it can also regenerate vitamin E, vitamin C and coenzyme Q_{10}. What this means is this: When your body runs out of vitamin E, vitamin C or coenzyme Q_{10}, lipoic acid actually restores them to their full antioxidant power.

Not only is lipoic acid a powerful aid against high blood pressure, but it also helps control blood sugar and insulin levels. As we already saw, these are often associated with hypertension.

If you have high blood pressure, take 100 milligrams of lipoic acid twice a day.

B complex

B_{12}, B_6 and folic acid play a vital role in protecting your blood vessels from toxic substances.

Here's how it works: Homocysteine is a very toxic amino acid. It creates tremendous amounts of free radicals that wreak havoc on your artery linings, thus opening the door to blood clots and atherosclerosis.

Normally your body converts this dangerous substance into other beneficial amino acids, either methionine or cysteine. But if you do not get enough folic acid, B_{12} and B_6 through what you eat or by taking supplements, then your body can no longer convert homocysteine to the nontoxic amino acids methionine and cysteine. When homocysteine builds up in your body, it becomes extremely toxic to your blood vessels. That's where supplementation can help.

To return your homocysteine levels to normal, daily take:

- 800 mcg. of folic acid
- 50 mcg. of B_{12}
- 50 mg. of B_6

These dosages of B-complex vitamins are found in most comprehensive multivitamin formulas.

Arginine

Arginine is an amino acid that your body must have to manufacture the gas nitric oxide. Why is that important? Well, nitric oxide is important for a number of reasons. This gas is released by endothelial cells, which are the cells that line the arteries. Nitric oxide is a powerful vasodilator that lowers blood pressure by relaxing the smooth muscle cells of the arteries. It also prevents cells from attaching to the arterial walls. Your body makes its own nitric oxide from the amino acid arginine.

Take 1000–2000 milligrams of arginine three times a day to effectively lower blood pressure. Take it with a small amount of carbohydrates, and avoid eating meats or any other proteins since they will interfere with its absorption.

Celery

Celery is a truly natural alternative high blood pressure treatment. This wonder veggie contains a compound that lowers blood pressure. In fact, it lowers blood pressure in animals by 12 to 14 percent. It is also lowers cholesterol by about 7 percent.

I place all my patients with hypertension on four stalks of celery per day. This alone has been able to lower blood pressure to normal levels in many of my patients.

Garlic and onions

You can also beat high blood pressure by supplementing your diet with garlic and onions. Garlic contains adenosine, which is a smooth muscle relaxant able to decrease blood pressure.

In a sixteen-week study, about forty patients with mild hypertension were given 600 milligrams of garlic three times a day. At the end of four weeks they experienced a 10 percent drop in systolic blood pressure, and at the end of sixteen weeks this drop in systolic blood pressure had plummeted to an amazing 19 percent.[2]

You can supplement your diet with garlic in several ways. Of course, you can eat fresh cloves or garlic juice, oil or powder. But if you don't enjoy the taste of garlic that much, you can even purchase garlic tablets.

Eating one to two raw garlic cloves a day is usually effective. Tablets should contain at least 400 milligrams of garlic. You should take one tablet three times a day.

Critical Minerals

For over twenty years Americans with hypertension have been warned to limit sodium in their diets. Numerous studies have confirmed that a low-sodium diet lowers blood pressure if you are "sodium sensitive."[3]

Sodium controls the amount of fluid outside the cells and regulates the body's water balance and blood volume. Your kidneys actually regulate the amount of sodium in your body. When your sodium level is low, your kidneys begin to conserve sodium. When levels become high, your kidneys excrete the excess sodium in the urine.

Salt is the most common source of sodium. It is made up of approximately 60 percent chloride and 40 percent sodium. Your body requires about 500 milligrams of sodium every day, which is approximately a quarter of a teaspoon of salt. But Americans consume between 3000 and 4000 milligrams a day.

Too much sodium causes the body to retain water, so your blood volume increases. The increased volume of blood then forces the heart to work harder, leading to increased resistance in the arteries, which in turn leads to high blood pressure.

The Power of Potassium

Potassium is another mineral that helps to lower blood pressure. It also helps to keep your body's sodium level down to acceptable levels. That's why eating foods high in potassium, such as fresh fruits and vegetables, can protect against high blood pressure.

Look for these high potassium foods when you grocery shop:

- Beans (especially lima beans and soybeans)
- Tomatoes
- Prunes
- Avocados
- Bananas
- Peaches
- Cantaloupes

Also, a form of seaweed called dulse is extremely high in potassium. More than 4000 milligrams of potassium are found in one-sixth of a cup! You can find dulse at your favorite health food store.

Magnificent Magnesium

Magnesium is vital for healthy blood pressure and a robust cardiovascular system. This powerful mineral is linked to more than 325 different enzyme reactions. If your body is deficient in magnesium, you could be predisposed to developing hypertension, arrhythmias and other cardiovascular conditions. Magnificent magnesium actually dilates arteries, thus decreasing blood pressure.

Are you magnesium deficient?

Many Americans are woefully lacking in magnesium. As a matter of fact, it is one of the most common deficiencies in the country, especially for the elderly.

Why? We drink too much coffee and alcohol, and we eat too many processed foods, all of which rob our bodies of this important mineral. For this reason I strongly recommend taking a magnesium supplement.

Take 400 milligrams of a chelated form such as magnesium glycinate, magnesium citrate or magnesium aspartate once or twice a day.

Common sources of magnesium include nuts and seeds, green leafy vegetables, legumes and whole grains. Let me caution you, however, that too much magnesium may cause diarrhea.

Incredible Calcium

Did you know that the most abundant mineral in your body is calcium? Calcium is critically important for maintaining the balance between your sodium and potassium and for regulating your blood pressure.

You can increase the amount of calcium in your diet by eating the following calcium-rich foods:

- Almonds
- Skim milk
- Skim milk cheeses
- Low-fat yogurt
- Sunflower seeds
- Soy
- Parsley
- Low-fat cottage cheese

Or try taking a daily calcium supplement. Take

500 milligrams of chelated calcium citrate twice a day.

A Stress-Busting Cocktail

Finally, nutritional supplements are powerful stress busters. Stress, as you know, is a major factor in high blood pressure. We will look more closely at the link between stress and high blood pressure later on. For now, here's a list of powerful supplements that can reduce the harmful effects of stress upon your cardiovascular system.

A multivitamin/multimineral supplement

Take a good, comprehensive multivitamin and mineral supplement every day, such as Divine Health Multivitamin.

B complex

I also recommend extra B complex.

Korean ginseng

Take 250 milligrams of Korean ginseng two to three times a day.

DHEA

Men, take 50 milligrams of DHEA one to two times a day. Have your doctor check your DHEA level and PSA before starting this supplement.

Pregnenolone

Women, take 30–100 milligrams of pregnenolone once or twice a day.

Phosphatidyl serine

Phosphatidyl serine is an amino acid that helps to decrease cortisol levels. Take 100 milligrams one to three times a day.

You may also try glandular adrenal formulas such as DSF Formula from Nutri-West. This supplement helps to restore adrenal function.

If you continue to feel really stressed out, get evaluated by your doctor. Sometimes excessive stress is related to chronic depression and chronic anxiety.

The Wonders of Water

Believe it or not, the best nutrient you can take for controlling your blood pressure is water.

When your body is lacking water, the water volume in every cell will be reduced, which then affects how efficiently nutrients and waste products are transported. What happens in the end is that our cells don't get enough nutrients, and they end up having too much waste collecting in the cells.

In addition, when you don't have enough water, your kidneys reabsorb more sodium.

After you do drink fluids, this sodium in turn attracts and holds even more water, making the blood volume increase, which may in turn increase your blood pressure.

If you don't drink enough water for too long, your body will begin to make certain adjustments to keep blood flowing to your brain, heart, kidneys, liver and lungs. Blood will be shunted away from less-essential tissues and sent to the vital organs. Your body will actually divert water by constricting small arteries that lead to less-essential tissues. In other words, your body will begin a water rationing program to make sure that enough blood goes to the vital organs first.

Think of it like this: When you constrict a water hose by bending it or by pressing your thumb over the opening, what happens? The

> *God remains the strength of my heart; he is mine forever.*
> —PSALM 73:26

pressure behind that constriction increases dramatically, doesn't it? Your arteries behave in a similar way. Therefore, increasing your intake of water helps to open up your arteries and helps to prevent this rise in blood pressure.

Often an individual with elevated blood pressure is placed on medication when all he really needs is a drink of water. When high blood pressure is detected early enough, simply drinking two to three quarts of filtered water a day can usually bring it back to normal.

What's even worse than medicating a person who just needs water is placing such an individual on diuretics, which happens all the time.

Eight glasses of water a day keep high blood pressure away

If you have high blood pressure, drink at least eight to twelve glasses of filtered water a day. The best time to drink water is thirty minutes before meals and two hours after meals. However, if you have kidney disease or a weak heart, you will need to limit your water intake. You should be under the care of a physician.

Hypertension Medications

The best way to control your blood pressure is through changes in diet and lifestyle, increasing your water intake, taking the nutritional supplements and minerals, reducing stress and decreasing your weight. But if after doing all the above you find that your blood pressure is still elevated, you may need the help of medication. Realize, however, that all hypertensive medications may have side effects. About twenty million Americans now take medicines to lower their blood pressure. It's critically important to work with your doctor and find a medicine that's right for you.

In addition, if you have high blood pressure, I strongly recommend that you visit a nutritional doctor— either a nutritional

> *And now, in my old age, don't set me aside. Don't abandon me when my strength is failing.*
> —PSALM 71:9

medical doctor, a doctor of osteopathy or a naturopath who can use stress reduction, weight control, nutritional therapy, aerobic exercise and adequate water intake as a first line of therapy for controlling hypertension.

Conclusion

Supplements, nutrients, water, stress reduction, diet and lifestyle changes and weight reduction can powerfully strengthen your body against the ravages of high blood pressure. But your greatest source of strength is God Himself. The Bible says that those who look to Him for strength will not be disappointed. "How blessed is the man whose strength is in Thee; in whose heart are the highways to Zion . . . They go from strength to strength" (Ps. 84:5, 7, NAS).

Would you like to feel as if you go from strength to strength, blasting through every obstacle you encounter with God's power and might? If so, always look to God for your strength, wisdom, power and understanding. As the Creator of your very unique body, He will lead you to supplements, nutrients and everything else your body needs to lower your blood pressure and live strong past the threescore and ten years that we are all promised.

A BIBLE CURE PRAYER FOR YOU

Dear God, I thank You that You've created me to be the object of Your great love and affection. Be my strength every day of my life, and let me live to go from strength to strength. Thank You for being a shield and protector for my life and health. Thank You for providing strength and help for my body. I pray for the power of discipline to be faithful to all of the wisdom You are teaching me through this booklet. Amen.

A BIBLE CURE PRESCRIPTION

Describe the changes you plan to make after reading this chapter.

_____

_____

_____

The Bible says that God is your protector and your shield. How does that apply personally to your own situation of high blood pressure?

_____

_____

_____

Do you believe that God is a healer? Why?

_____

_____

_____

_____

Chapter 5

Building Strength Through Dynamic Faith

I'd like to share with you one of the most powerful scriptures in the Bible. It says, "The eyes
of the LORD search the whole earth in order to
strengthen those whose hearts are fully com-
mitted to him" (2 Chron. 16:9).

What this means is this: When you commit
your heart to God, He is always looking for ways
to make you stronger—and He has the entire
earth at His disposal. This is important because it
means that you can trust God to strengthen your
body and your life, even against a physical assault
of high blood pressure.

God's eye is on the sparrow. The Bible says,
"What is the price of five sparrows? A couple of
pennies? Yet God does not forget a single one of
them. And the very hairs on your head are all
numbered. So don't be afraid; you are more

valuable to him than a whole flock of sparrows"
(Luke 12:6–7).

Not a tiny sparrow flies through the sky that
God doesn't watch over. If He sees them and cares
deeply for their every need, how much more does
He watch over you? He cares for your every
need—the needs of your body, your mind and
your spirit.

Having faith in God's unwav-
ering love for you is the last
Bible cure key to freedom
from high blood pressure.

> *With
> his stripes we
> are healed.*
> —Isaiah 53:5, kjv

Before we look more closely at this key, I want
to take a moment and discuss what faith is.

Many people believe that faith is some eerie
power that some have while others do not.
That's simply not true. Faith is nothing more
than a choice to believe God and take Him at His
Word—the Bible. Faith in action makes the
choice to believe God no matter what the circumstances say, no matter what your feelings
and emotions say, no matter what your friends
say. Faith looks beyond the natural realm and
touches the supernatural when it chooses to
believe. It's really so simple!

58

Faith for All That Concerns You

Some people believe that they can have faith for salvation, but otherwise they feel that God has pretty much left them on their own. But if God cares deeply for a tiny sparrow, and if He has numbered all the hairs on your head, do you really think He doesn't care about your other health issues? Of course He does. He cares greatly about all of them—even your high blood pressure!

I believe that is why God has led me to write this and other Bible Cure booklets, because God truly does care very deeply about you and your health. He is a wonderful Creator who created your body to function well for you. He also wants you to have the necessary wisdom and understanding to keep it functioning well for a very long time. Good health—that's God's plan for you because He loves you. Don't ever forget, you are the apple of His eye! He even wishes above all things that you prosper and be in *health*, even as your soul prospers. (See 3 John 2.)

God's Love and Your Health

Understanding God's love for you can have a powerful impact upon your health. When you truly begin to trust God for the many details of your life, you will begin to discover a peace in your life that has many powerful benefits to your soul, your mind and, yes, to your health. When you know how much God loves you, you will rest from the anxious striving and worry of life. Not only will you be happier, but you will also be much healthier. For stress has a profoundly negative impact upon you, especially upon your blood pressure. Let's take a look.

Stress and Your Health

Stress can raise your blood pressure. Dr. Hans Selye discussed two types of stress—*eustress* and *distress*.[1] Eustress is good stress, such as falling in love, that motivates and inspires. Distress is bad stress and can be short-lived or chronic. Dr. Selye observed that if a situation is perceived as very good or very bad, then demands are placed upon the mind and the body accordingly to adapt to the situation.

Not all stress is harmful, and some degree of stress is actually necessary to stay healthy. But stress becomes chronic and is very detrimental to our bodies when we believe we have lost control and therefore give up. Some life-events that can cause chronic stress are listed as follows:

- Unexpected illness

- Accidents
- Divorce or separation
- Loss of job
- Lawsuit
- Financial stress

Really, any stress that produces the following emotions qualifies as chronic stress:

- Feelings of loss
- Emotional distress
- Hostility
- Bereavement
- Chronic anxiety
- Depression
- Hopelessness
- Defeat

Chronic stress has been directly linked to a vast array of illnesses, including high blood pressure, heart disease, cancer, a suppressed immune system, chronic fatigue, headaches, insomnia, depression and anxiety.

Chronic anger and depression that often accompany chronic stress increase your risk of both heart attack and stroke.

Dr. Selye experimented with rats using different physical stressors such as electrical shocks and cold temperature. By doing this he discovered that if stress was maintained long enough, the body would go through three stages. These stages include the alarm stage, the resistance stage and the exhaustion stage.

Stage One: Alarm

In the early 1900s Dr. Walter Cannon of Harvard University first coined the phrase "fight-or-flight response." This is now known as the stress response, which is a kind of intricate and elaborate emergency alarm system that God created in your body. It is actually a survival response placed in us by God for our protection.

The fight-or-flight response actually begins in the hypothalamus, which is an area of the brain involved in survival. When you encounter a dangerous situation, such as being attacked by a bear, your hypothalamus signals your pituitary gland to secrete a hormone that in turn activates the adrenal glands. These glands release adrenaline, which is epinephrine. I'm sure you've heard someone say that he was operating on adrenaline. This is what that person was referring to.

This fight-or-flight response signals massive changes. Your entire body goes on high alert.

- Your muscles tighten and get tense.
- Your heart rate increases.
- Your blood vessels constrict.
- Your blood pressure rises.
- Breathing becomes faster and deeper.
- Perspiration increases.
- Blood is shunted away from the stomach so that digestion is slowed or halted.
- Blood sugar is dumped into the bloodstream for extra energy.
- Fats rise in the blood.
- The thyroid gland is stimulated.
- The secretion of saliva is slowed down.
- The brain becomes more alert.
- Sensory perception becomes sharper.

This alarm reaction can save your life. If you see a rattlesnake while hiking, you are able to run to safety. If you're camping and get attacked by a bear, you can get away and survive. This incredible alarm system may allow you to escape from disaster by secreting these powerful hormones that provide tremendous strength and energy.

We have all heard the accounts of the grandmother who lifted a car off of her elderly husband after the jack slipped and the car pinned him underneath. Fantastic though they sound, these stories are true. They reveal the power of this incredible stress system to respond to danger.

I actually had one patient who was car-jacked. As she was being driven to a remote area, she jumped out of the car as it was moving and was able to run to safety. This survival response that God placed in us for our protection works in similar fashion to the passing gear in a car. It empowers us with a burst of near superhuman power and strength in order to overcome adversity by fighting or fleeing.

The Problem of Modern Stress

This powerful defense system once served us well. It took our ancestors across the prairies, through attacks by enemies, pestilence, natural disasters and more and helped them to forge this land into the civilized nation we now enjoy.

But modern life is very different. Modern attacks don't come from wild animals and hostile tribesmen. Today psychological or emotional enemies that are no less real than the wild bears that attacked our forefathers threaten our lives. But the nature of modern stress poses a challenge to our bodies.

Modern psychological and emotional stress is

far more constant and continuous than an occasional bear attack. The activities of fighting or fleeing would have helped to dissipate the alarm reaction by burning off these stress chemicals and the sugar and fats that were released into the bloodstream. However, when the alarm response occurs continually throughout the day from emotional or psychological stresses or for insignificant events, our body gets bombarded with powerful stress chemicals that have no outlet.

Stage Two: Resistance

If the body's alarm response becomes more and more frequent, it leads to the second stage of stress, which is known as the resistance stage. This, again, is a natural survival response placed in us by God to help us survive without adequate nutrition, as during times of famine, war and pestilence.

In 2 Kings 25:1–4 we read about a siege upon the Jews by Babylon that lasted for one and a half years. During this time the people lacked food. These ancient citizens of Jerusalem experienced this stage two survival response. This response begins when an individual perceives that he or she has lost control. In modern life it's seen when a person encounters considerable financial stress with no way out, seriously failing health, the loss of a job, divorce or separation or some other traumatic event where an individual perceives a long-term loss of control.

Gearing Up to Survive

Remember that during this second stage your body believes you have encountered some long-term crisis such as a war, famine or drought. It now begins sending powerful signals to all your systems to give you the best chance of survival, regardless of your circumstances.

So what happens at this stage?

- Your hypothalamus is stimulated.
- This in turn stimulates the pituitary gland.
- A prolonged increase of both the hormones cortisol and adrenaline are released.
- The cortisol actually causes a decreased sensitivity of the brain centers for feedback inhibition.
- This leads to prolonged elevation of cortisol.
- Blood sugar is elevated.

As your blood sugar level is increased over

time, insulin resistance can occur, leading to Type 2 diabetes. It also leads to increased bone loss, an elevation in blood fats such as triglycerides and cholesterol and an increased accumulation of fat, especially around the waist, leading to "apple-shaped obesity."

The resistance stage also leads to an increased breakdown of proteins that can cause muscle wasting, especially in the arms, legs and other large muscle groups. At this point your immune system can begin to falter and fail as the levels of immune cells become increasingly depleted.

During the resistance stage the prolonged increase of adrenaline and cortisol leads to a loss of magnesium, potassium and calcium. These minerals are extremely important for blood pressure control. Without them blood pressure usually remains elevated. As the levels of both cortisol and adrenaline remain high, hypertension and heart disease can result.

Stage Three: Exhaustion

As the body activates the sympathetic nervous system over such a long period of time without giving it a break, eventually the adrenal glands become depleted. The two powerful hormones that started and sustained this process for so long now begin to become depleted. Both cortisol and adrenaline levels decline.

When Your Body Cannot Go Anymore

Your body has launched and sustained all of its resources for a very long time. Now it simply begins to wear out—and sometimes it can wear out rather quickly. Think about it in this way: Imagine getting into your car and pressing the gas petal to the floor for hours while the car is in park with its engine running. No doubt it would take quite a toll on the engine. Now think about what would happen to the engine if you sustained this for days or weeks. It wouldn't be long before the engine began to break down in significant ways.

When your body is forced to deal with the biochemical storm created by stress for a sustained period of time, the same thing occurs—your once robust, powerful body that was designed to last for many, many years begins to break down prematurely.

If you are a stressed-out person in stage three exhaustion, here's what you might expect. You may begin to experience hypoglycemia, which is low blood sugar. In addition, poor fat and protein absorption in your body could lead to the loss of muscle mass.

With time, your immune system will become depleted, and you may experience some of the following symptoms:

- Allergies
- Inflammation and joint aches and pains
- Lower resistance to infection
- Severe fatigue
- Anxiety
- Irritability
- Memory problems

During this stage you can be very susceptible to infections (bacterial and viral infections such as chronic sinusitis, recurrent bronchitis and pharyngitis), allergies (environmental and food), autoimmune diseases (such as rheumatoid arthritis, lupus, thyroiditis and multiple sclerosis) and cancer. Organ systems may also begin to fail during this stage.

Dealing With
Modern Stress at the Roots

Since today's stress generally has a large psycho-logical and emotional component, getting it under control so that it cannot overdrive the body's organ systems requires hitting it at the roots.

Long-term stress is rooted in the perception that you've lost control. Therefore, to manage stress it is critical that you develop a perception of control over your life. Studies have found that individuals with excessive stress on the job have more hypertension.[2] But it's not really the stress. Two people can encounter the same circumstances, and one may be overwhelmed with stress while the other one remains completely undisturbed. It's not actually stress of the work, but the perception of loss of control that causes blood pressure to rise.

The Power of God's Word Over Stress

You are much more than a body—you are body, mind, emotions and spirit. And I've learned that in order to treat you effectively, I must pay attention to all of your needs: physical, mental, emotional and spiritual. Since stress is rooted in the perception of loss of control, renewing your mind with the Word of God will yank up stress by the roots. In other words, stress begins in the mind, and the Word of God has the power to shield, protect and strengthen the mind against the power of stress.

The Bible is much more than just a wise story. It contains living words of truth and power spoken by a living God

> *He heals the brokenhearted, binding up their wounds.*
> —PSALM 147:3

who loves you and longs to see you walk in wholeness and health. Here are some powerful scriptures from God's living Word for you. I encourage you to think about them, meditate upon them, pray about them, memorize them and most importantly, choose to believe them!

When you feel stressed out, look up Galatians 5:16–26 to help you take control of your thoughts.

> So I advise you to live according to your new life in the Holy Spirit. Then you won't be doing what your sinful nature craves. The old sinful nature loves to do evil, which is just opposite from what the Holy Spirit wants. And the Spirit gives us desires that are opposite from what the sinful nature desires. These two forces are constantly fighting each other, and your choices are never free from this conflict. But when you are

directed by the Holy Spirit, you are no longer subject to the law.

When you follow the desires of your sinful nature, your lives will produce these evil results: sexual immorality, impure thoughts, eagerness for lustful pleasure, idolatry, participation in demonic activities, hostility, quarreling, jealousy, outbursts of anger, selfish ambition, divisions, the feeling that everyone is wrong except those in your own little group, envy, drunkenness, wild parties, and other kinds of sin. Let me tell you again, as I have before, that anyone living that sort of life will not inherit the Kingdom of God.

But when the Holy Spirit controls our lives, he will produce this kind of fruit in us: love, joy, peace, patience, kindness, goodness, faithfulness, gentleness, and self-control. Here there is no conflict with the law.

Those who belong to Christ Jesus have nailed the passions and desires of their sinful nature to his cross and crucified them there. If we are living now by the Holy Spirit, let us follow the Holy Spirit's leading in every part of our lives. Let us

not become conceited, or irritate one
another, or be jealous of one another.

Controlling Every Thought

The Bible promises us that we can control every
anxious, worried, fretful and fearful thought.
We don't have to let stress get the upper hand in
our minds.

Here's a powerful scripture to read aloud
when stress begins to assault your thoughts:

> Casting down imaginations, and every high
> thing that exalteth itself against the knowl-
> edge of God, and bringing into captivity
> every thought to the obedience of Christ.
>
> —2 Corinthians 10:5, KJV

You have fought back against your stress-filled
thoughts with God's Word. Now you must fill your
mind with God's thoughts to protect it with the
power of God's peace. Here's an important verse
to memorize and obey.

> Finally, brethren, whatever things are
> true, whatever things are noble, what-
> ever things are just, whatever things are
> pure, whatever things are lovely, what-
> ever things are of good report, if there is

any virtue and if there is anything praise-
worthy—meditate on these things.

—Philippians 4:8, NKJV

In addition to thinking about what is pure,
lovely and honest, I also encourage you to begin
memorizing scriptures. Write the following verses
on notecards and keep them with you throughout
the day. Pull them out at lunch or when you are
waiting in line or riding a bus. You will find that
they will come back into your mind at important
moments and will guard your mind from stress.

Study this Book of the Law continually.
Meditate on it day and night so you may
be sure to obey all that is written in it.
Only then will you succeed.

—Joshua 1:8

For as he thinketh in his heart, so is he.

—Proverbs 23:7, KJV

Let this mind be in you, which was also
in Christ Jesus.

—Philippians 2:5, KJV

Thou wilt keep him in perfect peace,
whose mind is stayed on thee.

—Isaiah 26:3, KJV

> Be not conformed to this world: but be ye
> transformed by the renewing of your mind.
>
> —ROMANS 12:2, KJV

Taming the Power of the Tongue

In addition to taking control of your mind, you must also begin to tame your tongue. That may seem impossible at first, but it's not. God's Word also has power to help you begin saying only those thing that you won't regret later on. Thoughts and words are very closely connected. James 3:6 in the King James Version calls the tongue a fire, a world of iniquity. Like a fire, words can set destructive stress ablaze all around you.

In order to keep your mind free from stress, you must quit letting your words be the vehicles upon which stressful thoughts can travel.

Here are some powerful verses for you to memorize:

> Out of the abundance of the heart the
> mouth speaketh.
>
> —MATTHEW 12:34, KJV

> Every idle word that men shall speak,
> they shall give account thereof in the day
> of judgment.
>
> —MATTHEW 12:36, KJV

Let no corrupt communication proceed out of your mouth.

—Ephesians 4:29, kjv

Death and life are in the power of the tongue.

—Proverbs 18:21, kjv

The Power of Forgiveness

I've discovered that stress can anchor itself in a person's soul through grudges, old hurts, wounds and bitter feelings. Many people harbor hidden anger, bitterness, unforgiveness, resentment, fear, hatred, abandonment, shame and other deadly emotions that they aren't even aware of.

These hidden emotions can stress out your mind and elevate your blood pressure. This kind of stress

> *In your presence is fullness of joy.*
> —Psalm 16:11, nkjv

is impossible to remove except through the power of forgiveness. The Scriptures say, "Don't let the sun go down while you are still angry" (Eph. 4:26). In other words, release the anger and forgive, for if you don't, it will eventually develop into a hidden emotion, raise your blood pressure and wreak havoc on your body.

I encourage you to take stock of your own

heart right now. Are there people in your life whom you haven't forgiven? Do memories of old hurts and wounds surface in your thoughts when you encounter certain individuals? Have people hurt you in the past in ways that you just buried, but didn't really deal with?

Make up your mind right now, at this very moment, to release everybody and anybody from the hold you have over them through unforgiveness. You may say, "But you have no idea how much this person wronged me. This individual destroyed my life."

That's exactly why you must forgive that person. Unforgiveness doesn't punish the person who wronged you; it punishes you through stress and all of its destructive physical and mental assaults. You can be free from the stress created by unforgiveness by simply forgiving.

When I encounter situations in my own life for which forgiveness is needed but difficult, I simply reflect on how Christ felt on the cross. He forgave me and He forgave you—but His forgiveness for us was anything but easy. Ask Him to help you to forgive. He will. He will never fail you.

It's vital that you learn to practice the power of forgiveness. Mark 11:25–26 says, "Whenever you stand praying, if you have anything against anyone, forgive him, that your Father in heaven may also forgive you your trespasses. But if you do not forgive, neither will your Father in heaven forgive your trespasses" (NKJV).

Studies have actually shown that people who express their anger tend to have lower blood pressure. Therefore, it is critically important to forgive and to release these deadly emotions before they have a chance to take root and destroy your health.

Walking in the Power of Love

One of the greatest powers available to you is the power of love. It is truly supernatural and can save even the most bitter situation. The Bible says that love never fails. (See 1 Corinthians 13:8.)

We are commanded by Christ to walk in love and to enjoy the fruit of love's power in our lives. "So now I am giving you a new commandment: Love each other. Just as I have loved you, you should love each other. Your love for one another will prove to the world that you are my disciples" (John 13:34–35).

The power of love can free you of fear, which stress is often rooted in.

There is no fear in love; but perfect love
casteth out fear.

—1 John 4:18, kjv

Giving Love

Do you feel alone and needing love? We all need
love. You may find that one wonderful way to sur-
round your life with love is to own a loving pet.
When you get home from work, it will always be
there waiting, eager to see you and always by your
side. You may find that holding your adoring
animal on your lap causes the stress of your
hectic day to melt away.

You can't be selfish when you love, for love has
to be given away. And one of the best ways to
lower your stress is to give and receive love. Make
every effort to give away God's pure love. Hug
your spouse or a friend, hold hands with your
child, give an elderly person a loving touch.
Express the love of Christ often, and ask God for
opportunities to give His love away.

A Gift of Laughter

One of the greatest gifts you cultivate in your life is
the gift of laughter. It's impossible to have a merry
heart and remain filled with resentment and

anger. Learn to practice a merry heart. The Bible says it works like medicine. "A merry heart does good, like medicine" (Prov. 17:22, NKJV).

Laughter releases chemicals in the brain that can help to relieve pain and create a sense of well-being. Laughter also strengthens the heart, lungs and muscles. In fact, Norman Cousins referred to laughter as internal jogging.[3] Just twenty seconds of laughter produces an exchange of oxygen equal to about twenty minutes of aerobic exercise.

I believe laughter is the best medicine for relieving stress and hypertension. If you are stressed out or depressed, or if you have high blood pressure, learn to laugh. Cultivate laughter in your life. Go to funny movies, watch funny, clean TV shows, tell jokes, get joke books and read comic sections in the newspaper. Laughter is truly the best medicine for overcoming stress.

Conclusion

By now I trust you realize that high blood pressure is not a life sentence. I believe that you will overcome high blood pressure and go forward to develop a healthier lifestyle in many ways.

It's so important to follow the God-established principles of good health. But it's far more important to know and follow Jesus Christ. If all of this discussion about the love of God seems vague and distant to you, I'd like to invite you to get to know Christ in a more personal way. All you need to do is pray to Him, ask His forgiveness for your sins and invite Him into your heart and into your life. He's so close to you right now—He's only a prayer away. Knowing Him is the greatest privilege and blessing you will ever experience. Why not pray with me right now?

A BIBLE CURE PRAYER FOR YOU

Dear Jesus, I would like to know You better, to know the power of Your love and the peace of Your presence in my life. I give You my heart and my life, and I ask You to forgive me for all my sins. Teach me to walk in Your ways according to Your wonderful wisdom and mighty grace. Thank You for dying to save me and to heal me. In Your name, amen.

R BIBLE CURE PRESCRIPTION

How do you plan to begin to cultivate a merry heart? (circle one)

Reading funny books
Telling jokes
Watching funny movies
All of the above

If you prayed the prayer asking Christ into your heart, write your own prayer thanking Him for saving you.

_____

_____

_____

_____

_____

_____

_____

Conclusion

You now have a powerful plan to combat high blood pressure that addresses your total person—body, mind and spirit. The wisdom you have received through this booklet isn't mine. It comes from God, from His Word and from the knowledge He has given to help you to live well and healthy. Now this Bible cure belongs to you.

As you begin making changes to your lifestyle, never forget the power of prayer to change your life. God is always as close as the whisper of a prayer. Pray often throughout your day, asking Him for help in every circumstance. He will not disappoint you. Draw strength from His wonderful Word every day. By faith I believe that you will walk in divine health from this day on. Your best days are ahead of you!

—Don Colbert, M.D.

Notes

CHAPTER 3
BUILDING STRENGTH THROUGH
EXERCISE AND LIFESTYLE CHANGES

1   American College of Sports Medicine, "Position Stand Physical Activity, Physical Fitness and Hypertension," *Medical Science Sports Exercise 10* (1993): i–x.

2.   "Physical Activity and Health: A Report of the Surgeon General, Atlanta," U.S. Department of Health and Human Services, Centers for Disease Control and Prevention, National Center for Chronic Disease Prevention and Health Promotion (1996).

3.   R. R. Pate et al., "Physical Activity and Public Health," *Journal of the American Medical Association* 273 (1995): 402–407.

CHAPTER 4
BUILDING STRENGTH THROUGH SUPPLEMENTS

1.   M. J. Stampfer et al., "Vitamin E Consumption and the Risk of Coronary Disease in Women," *New England Journal of Medicine* 328 (1993): 1430.

2.   O. S. de Santos et al., "Effects of Garlic Powder and Garlic Oil Preparations on Blood Lipids, Blood Pressure and Well-Being," *BR J Res* 6 (1995): 91–100.

3.   F. C. Luft et al., "Sodium Intake and Essential Hypertension," *Hypertension* 4(5) (1982): 14–19.

Chapter 5
Building Strength Through Dynamic Faith

1. Hans Selye, *The Stress of Life* (New York: McGraw-Hill, 1956).

2. T. Pickering, "Tension and Hypertension," *Journal of the American Medical Association* 370 (1993): 2494.

3. Norman Cousins, *Anatomy of an Illness As Perceived by the Patient* (New York: Bantam, 1981).

Don Colbert, M.D., was born in Tupelo, Mississippi. He attended Oral Roberts School of Medicine in Tulsa, Oklahoma, where he received a bachelor of science degree in biology in addition to his degree in medicine. Dr. Colbert completed his internship and residency with Florida Hospital in Orlando, Florida. He is board certified in family practice and has received extensive training in nutritional medicine.

If you would like more
information about natural and
divine healing, or information about
Divine Health Nutritional Products®,
you may contact
Dr. Colbert at:

Dr. Don Colbert

1908 Boothe Circle
Longwood, FL 32750
Telephone: 407-331-7007

Dr. Colbert's website is
www.drcolbert.com.

Pick up these other Siloam Press
books by Dr. Colbert:

Walking in Divine Health

What You Don't Know May Be Killing You

The Bible Cure® Booklet Series
The Bible Cure for ADD and Hyperactivity
The Bible Cure for Allergies
The Bible Cure for Arthritis
The Bible Cure for Cancer
The Bible Cure for Candida and Yeast Infection
The Bible Cure for Chronic Fatigue and Fibromyalgia
The Bible Cure for Depression and Anxiety
The Bible Cure for Diabetes
The Bible Cure for Headaches
The Bible Cure for Heart Disease
The Bible Cure for Heartburn and Indigestion
The Bible Cure for High Blood Pressure
The Bible Cure for Memory Loss
The Bible Cure for Menopause
The Bible Cure for Osteoporosis
The Bible Cure for PMS and Mood Swings
The Bible Cure for Sleep Disorders
The Bible Cure for Weight Loss and Muscle Gain

SILOAM PRESS
A part of Strang Communications Company
600 Rinehart Road
Lake Mary, FL 34726
(800) 599-5750